A Song of Worship

Written By: Terri Etheridge
Illustrated By: Sandra Townes

A Song of Worship, by Terri Etheridge©2021

ISBN: 9798713044992

I will sing of your GREAT Love oh, Lord
I will sing of your GREAT Love oh, Lord

I will sing of your GREAT Love oh, Lord
Forever, and ever, and ever!

APOSTOLIC
EXPRESS
ON TRACK
WITH GOD
OBEY
GOD'S WAY

I will CLAP my hands to you oh, Lord
I will CLAP my hands to you oh, Lord
I will CLAP my hands to you oh, Lord
Forever, and ever, and ever!

I will sing of your GREAT Love oh, Lord
I will sing of your GREAT Love oh, Lord
Fresh Baked Goods daily!

I will sing of your GREAT Love oh, Lord
Forever, and ever, and ever!
GRAND OPENING

I will JUMP and give you praise oh, Lord
I will JUMP and give you praise oh, Lord

I will JUMP and give you praise oh, Lord
Forever, and ever, and ever!

I will sing of your GREAT Love oh, Lord
I will sing of your GREAT Love oh, Lord

I will sing of your GREAT Love oh, Lord
Forever, and ever, and ever!

2 3 4 5 6 7 8 9 10 11 12 13 14 15 16 17 18 19 20 21 22 2

I will DANCE and give you praise oh, Lord
I will DANCE and give you praise oh, Lord

I will DANCE and give you praise oh, Lord
Forever, and ever, and ever!

I will sing of your GREAT Love oh, Lord
I will sing of your GREAT Love oh, Lord

I will sing of your GREAT Love oh, Lord
Forever, and ever, and ever!

I will wave my arms in praise oh, Lord
I will wave my arms in praise oh, Lord

I will wave my arms in praise oh, Lord
Forever, and ever, and ever!

I will sing of your GREAT Love oh, Lord
I will sing of your GREAT Love oh, Lord
I will sing of your GREAT Love oh, Lord
Forever, and ever, and ever!

CHRISTMAS
FESTIVAL

For you alone are worthy Lord,
For you alone are worthy Lord,

SEASONS
SUMMER
SPRING
AUTUMN
CALENDAR
Solar System
ALPHABET
NUMBERS
BLAST OFF
to the 100th day!
For you alone are worthy Lord,
Forever, and ever, and ever!